UNLOCKING
THE SECRETS
OF THE FEASTS

 ————————————————

THE PROPHECIES IN THE FEASTS OF LEVITICUS

MICHAEL NORTEN

WestBow
PRESS
A DIVISION OF THOMAS NELSON

WestBow Press books may be ordered through booksellers or by contacting:

WestBow Press
A Division of Thomas Nelson
1663 Liberty Drive
Bloomington, IN 47403
www.westbowpress.com
1-(866) 928-1240

ISBN: 978-1-4497-3410- 7 (sc)
ISBN: 978-1-4497-3409-1 (e)

Library of Congress Control Number: 2011962733

Printed in the United States of America

WestBow Press rev. date: 3/6/2012

CONTENTS

Spring Feasts {

Fall Feasts {

Fulfilled at Christ's 1st Coming

Will be fulfilled at Christ's 2nd Coming

ACKNOWLEDGMENTS

I want to thank Dr. Roy Zuck, Senior Professor Emeritus at Dallas Theological Seminary, for the initial editing of the text and Dr. John Reed, Senior Professor Emeritus of Pastoral Ministries at Dallas Theological Seminary, for his advice and encouragement. I am also grateful for the additional encouragement received from my wife, Ann.

This book is dedicated to the memory of my mother, Nadine Norten, who was very interested in the subject of the feasts of Leviticus and Bible prophecy.

PREFACE

When I was a college student, I took advantage of an opportunity to take a train ride to Mexico City with a number of other students during the Christmas holiday. Some people warned me that desperadoes liked to rob people on trains in Mexico, so I needed to be on guard. Obviously for a young college student that piece of information caused a great deal of imagination and concern. But by the time I was on the train, leaving Laredo, Texas, my concerns were mostly replaced by excitement and adventure. The train ride took two very long days to get all the way to Mexico City, so by the second day those warnings began to weigh on my mind. I was very much on the alert, sizing up every stranger I encountered. I happened to notice a gentleman who looked a little rough around the edges, probably from the long ride. While thinking that he looked a little suspicious to me, I chuckled to myself, because I remembered an episode in *The Lucy Show* in which Lucy was on a train ride and thought she spotted a suspicious person. She caused all kinds of problems, when she thought the innocent gentleman was a train robber.

As I was watching this man and his stern countenance, several people started gathering around with much interest. Being a curious young man, I decided to slowly move closer to the gathering to see if I could hear what they were talking about. I was startled to find that they were talking about the second coming of Christ! They were discussing the signs of the times and how things were lining up for Christ's imminent return. I enthusiastically joined the discussion, spilling out loads of questions. As we finally pulled into Mexico City, I thanked this gentleman and introduced myself to him. He shook my hand and introduced himself as Hal Lindsey. He later wrote the best seller *The Late Great Planet Earth*. Since that wonderful encounter, I have been studying Bible prophecy. And following Hal's recommendation, I attended Dallas Theological Seminary. I became so intrigued by how explicitly God orchestrated His plans for mankind and His itinerary for the ages.

While I was still a seminary student, one warm Sunday afternoon I decided to go for a pizza lunch with some of my friends after church. We entered a place called Shakey's Pizza. Little did I know that that lunch would set me up for a long and exciting journey of biblical discovery. The restaurant was designed so that everyone sat together, strangers and all, on benches at long tables. A nice baldheaded gentleman sat right across from me. I noticed an odd phenomenon about this man. It appeared that smoke was coming up from the back of his head. When I gently brought that to his attention, he turned as red as a beet and sheepishly brought out from behind his back a cigarette. He informed me that he was Jewish and had recently accepted Jesus as his Savior and Messiah. When he saw our group of churchgoers come in, he immediately tried to hide his cigarette, because he didn't know what Christians thought about smoking. We had a good laugh about it, and then we talked about the many evidences that convinced him that Jesus is the Messiah. Also to my delight, we talked about Christ's soon return. He was so much fun to talk with because he was very knowledgeable and humorous. This wonderful Jewish man turned out to be Zola Levitt. Later, he became a prolific writer and teacher. He told me something that stuck with me for years. He said that many of the secrets of God's plan for the ages were in the Levitical feasts. I kept thinking about that statement off and on for so long before I finally acted on it. Ever since then, I have had a nagging curiosity about the feasts. So recently I decided to research all that I could about them.

I thought it would be a good idea to seek insight from Jewish rabbis. I made inquiry with both messianic and orthodox rabbis. They all gave me a similar warning: "If you seriously study the feasts, you will experience a blessing that will be beyond your expectation." I appreciated the encouragement, and later I found out that they knew what they were talking about. They meant what they said. I have been blessed beyond my wildest dreams. I have been totally stunned at how much information God has packed into the observances of the seven feasts in Leviticus 23.

God opened several opportunities for me to teach what I had discovered about His seven feasts. God emphatically said in Leviticus 23:2 that these were His feasts that He designed for the Jews to observe and learn about Him. I noticed that the teaching about the feasts had the same effect on the people that I taught as it did me. They were greatly blessed by what God revealed about Himself in the observance of the feasts. I found that the information encourages, comforts, motivates, and strengthens one's faith.

One evening I was having dinner at a café in a hotel. To my delight I realized that Tim Lahaye, coauthor of the "Left Behind" series, was sitting at the next table. I took the opportunity to strike up a conversation with him and ask some questions about prophecy. The conversation got around to the feasts. When I shared with him some of the things I discovered from my visits with the rabbis and other sources, he was just as surprised at the information as I had been. He then encouraged me to write a book about my findings. As a result of his persuasion and encouragement, I decided to write this book, taking each feast one at a time and explaining them as I have discovered the mysteries unfold.

As you study the feasts with me, I hope that it will be a life-changing adventure, just as it has been for me.

INTRODUCTION

By the details of the feasts, both biblical and traditional, God revealed His plan for the ages. When you attend a concert or a play, you receive a printed program that tells you what and when each act will be performed. These seven feasts of God are His program laid out for us to know what is happening in the world. In studying the feasts, it became obvious to me that they fall into two different groups: the springs feasts and the fall feasts. These separate groupings are significant, and the timing between the feasts is important. The spring feasts picture the events surrounding Jesus Christ's first coming, and the fall feasts picture the events surrounding His second coming.

An important thing I noticed was that God said these feasts are His. In other words, they were not Israel's feasts, but His. Leviticus 23:1–2 reads, "The LORD spoke again to Moses, saying, 'Speak to the sons of Israel, and say to them, "The LORD's appointed times which you shall proclaim as holy convocations—My appointed times are these."'" God emphasized that these appointed times are His appointed times.

If we are to get an understanding of the times, we must become familiar with the Hebrew calendar. In our modern-day American culture, we are accustomed to the Gregorian calendar. This calendar is based on the sun, while the Hebrew calendar is based on the moon. This is why the dates of the feasts continue to float or appear at different days each year on our calendar.

The first two spring feasts are Passover (Pesach) and Unleavened Bread (Hag Ha Matzah). One follows immediately after the other because the Feast of Unleavened Bread is an extension of the Passover Feast. Leviticus 23:4–8 explains them in this way: "These are the appointed times of the LORD, holy convocations which you shall proclaim at the times appointed for them. In the first month, on the fourteenth day of the month at twilight is the LORD'S Passover. Then on the fifteenth day of the same month there is the Feast of Unleavened Bread to the LORD; for seven days you shall eat unleavened bread. On the first day you shall have a holy convocation; you shall not do any laborious work. But for seven days you shall present an offering by fire to the LORD. On the seventh day is a holy convocation; you shall not do any laborious work."

"The month" refers to the month of Abib, which was changed to Nisan after the Babylonian captivity. On our calendar it falls in March and April. Moses spoke to the people in Exodus 13:3–4: "And Moses said to the people, 'Remember this day in which you went out from Egypt, from the house of slavery; for by a powerful hand the LORD brought you out from this place. And nothing leavened shall be eaten. On this day in the month of Abib, you are about to go forth.'"

Then we come to the Feast of Firstfruits (Yom Bikkurim) in Leviticus 23:9–11:

9 "Then the LORD spoke to Moses, saying, 10 'Speak to the sons of Israel, and say to them, "When you enter the land which I am going to give to you and reap its harvest, then you shall bring in the sheaf of the firstfruits of your harvest to the priest. 11 And he shall wave the sheaf before the LORD for you to be accepted; on the day after the Sabbath the priest shall wave it."'"

The last of the spring feasts is the Feast of Pentecost. Since it is fifty days after Passover, it falls in May or June. The Hebrew name for the feast is Shavuot. In the Old Testament, the feast is called the Feast of Weeks, commemorating the giving of the Torah to Israel. Leviticus 23:15–16 says, 15 "You shall also count for yourselves from the day after the Sabbath, from the day when you brought in the sheaf of the wave offering; there shall be seven complete Sabbaths. 16 You shall count fifty days to the day after the seventh Sabbath; then you shall present a new grain offering to the LORD."

All four spring feasts have been fulfilled, as I will discuss later. There are three more feasts that have not been fulfilled, which are called the fall feasts. They are the Feast of Trumpets, the Day of Atonement, and the Feast of Tabernacles. These feasts fall in September and October on our Gregorian calendar.

The Feast of Trumpets (Rosh Hashanah) starts on the first day of Tishri, which is the seventh month of the sacred calendar, the Jewish New Year. Leviticus 23:23–25 says,

23 "Again the LORD spoke to Moses, saying, 24 'Speak to the sons of Israel, saying, "In the seventh month on the first of the month, you shall have a rest, a reminder by blowing of *trumpets*, a holy convocation. 25 You shall not do any laborious work, but you shall present an offering by fire to the LORD."'" The significance of this feast is quite startling. In a later chapter, I will discuss this very exciting feast. It may change your thinking about some things.

The Day of Atonement (Yom Kippur) is the tenth day of Tishri. It is a very solemn day for the Jews because it is judgment day. We read in Leviticus 23:26–32, 26 "And the LORD spoke to Moses, saying, 27 'On exactly the tenth day of this seventh month is the Day of Atonement; it shall be a holy convocation for you, and you shall humble your souls and present an offering by fire to the LORD. 28 Neither shall you do any work on this same day, for it is a day of atonement, to make atonement on your behalf before the LORD your God. 29 If there is any person who will not humble himself on this same day, he shall be cut off from his people. 30 As for any person who does any work on this same day, that person I will destroy from among his people. 31 You shall do no work at all. It is to be a perpetual statute throughout your generations in all your dwelling places. 32 It is to be a Sabbath of complete rest to you, and you shall humble your souls; on the ninth of the month at evening, from evening until evening you shall keep your Sabbath.'"

Finally, we come to the last of the fall feasts, the Feast of Tabernacles or Booths. This feast is to be observed on the fifteenth day of Tishri. This last feast is very festive because it occurs after the harvests have been completed, and God's gracious provisions are to be enjoyed with great celebration. Leviticus 23:33–36 reads, [33] "Again the LORD spoke to Moses, saying, [34] "Speak to the sons of Israel, saying, "On the fifteenth of this seventh month is the Feast of Booths for seven days to the LORD. [35] On the first day is a holy convocation; you shall do no laborious work of any kind. [36] For seven days you shall present an offering by fire to the LORD. On the eighth day you shall have a holy convocation and present an offering by fire to the LORD; it is an assembly. You shall do no laborious work.""""

You might notice that an eighth day follows the seven-day celebration, which seems somewhat strange. It turns out that this eighth day is very exciting in its significance to God's total plan of the ages. I will examine that also in a later chapter.

Keep in mind that four spring feasts have been fulfilled in the events relating to Christ's first coming, while the remaining three fall feasts are to be fulfilled by the events relating to His second coming.

THE HEBREW CALENDAR		
HEBREW (lunar-solar)	**LENGTH**	**GREGORIAN**
1 Nisan	30 days	March-April
2 Iyar	29 days	April-May
3 Sivan	30 days	May-June
4 Tammuz	29 days	June-July
5 Av	30 days	July-August
6 Elul	29 days	August-September
7 Tishri	30 days	September-October
8 Cheshvan	29 or 30 days	October-November
9 Kislev	30 or 29 days	November-December
10 Tevet	29 days	December-January
11 Shevat	30 days	January-February
12 Adar I (leap years only)	30 days	February-March
13 Adar (called Adar II in leap years)	29 days	February-March

 ———————————————————————————

Chapter 1

THE PASSOVER

The First of the Spring Feasts

THE FIRST PASSOVER

Many Christians are familiar with the events of the first Passover, but, when we study the particulars, we are confronted with some very interesting facts. When we read that God caused ten plagues to torment the Egyptians after the pharaoh stubbornly refused to let the Jews leave Egypt, we are tempted to just absorb the story and then move on to the next event. But God was doing much more to the Egyptians than just pressuring Pharaoh to release the Jews. He was teaching them about their many false gods and administering harsh judgment on their idolatry. As an example, when God turned the Nile to blood, He was attacking their worship of Khnum, their god of the river. Likewise, the next plague of frogs was an attack on Heqt, the frog-headed goddess of resurrection. She was the wife of Khnum. The other plagues were also attacks relating to other gods. Lice stopped their sacrifices because of cleanness issues, and swarms of flies were against Beelzebub, prince of the air, because flies were always flying around his ears. Livestock suffered disease for punishment against Apis, the sacred bull while boils were opposed to Imhotep, the god of medical cures. Hailstones showed the weakness of Nut, the sky goddess; locusts opposed Nepri, the grain god; darkness was an attack against Re, the sun god; and the death of the firstborn attacked all of the gods.

We read in Exodus 12:23, "This month shall be the beginning of months for you; it is to be the first month of the year to you. 'Speak to all the congregation of Israel, saying, 'On the tenth of this month they are each one to take a lamb for themselves, according to their fathers' households, a lamb for each household.'" The lamb was an attack on the Egyptian god Amon, the head of all their gods. He was presented in a human form, but his animal was a ram. The month of the Passover was also in the month of Nisan, the month when the Egyptians celebrated the deity of Amon.

I wondered if there was also any significance to taking a lamb on the tenth day of the month for the household. I became more curious when I read further in the Exodus passage. It reads in Exodus 12:6, "And you shall keep it until the fourteenth day of the same month, then the whole assembly of the congregation of Israel is to kill it at twilight." Why the fourteenth day? I discovered two very interesting answers. One, each day that the lamb was in captivity was to remind them of one hundred years of captivity in Egypt for a total of four hundred years. Two, for four days the lamb would become a pet to the family, so when it was sacrificed, they would know the gravity of the penalty of their sins. It is also important to note that the fourteenth was the full moon, which the Egyptians considered the pinnacle of Amon's power. Sacrificing the lamb demonstrated that Amon had no power at all.

We read further in Exodus 12:7: "Moreover, they shall take some of the blood and put it on the two doorposts and on the lintel of the houses in which they eat it." Many of us have heard that if you connected the spots of blood on the doorway, it would form a cross. I believe this is a legitimate observation, but I was sure that there were many more pictures which God provided for us. I visited with David Schiller, a teacher of the Torah at a messianic congregation, Eitz Chaim, in Richardson, Texas. He shared with me many interesting things about the Passover lamb. He explained that there is historical evidence that the lamb was roasted upright on a pomegranate pole with a crossbar through its shoulders. This obviously would bring to mind the cross. The pomegranate pole was used, because as a dry wood it would not boil. Boiling was prohibited in preparing the lamb. David mentioned another observation from tradition. The pomegranate is symbolic of royalty and the priesthood. Another interesting point is that the entrails were tied around the head so everything could be roasted evenly without boiling. This resembles the crown of thorns. Other sources verified David Schiller's descriptions. One very captivating article is "The Crucifixion of the Paschal Lamb," by Joseph Tabory, *Jewish Quarterly Review, New Series, Vol. 86 (Jan.–April 1996): 395–406.* Another good explanation of the parallels can be found in Alfred Edersheim's book, *The Temple: Its Ministry and Services,* chapter 12, "The Paschal Feast and the Lord's Supper."

We must remember that the feasts not only have historical teachings and spiritual implications but also prophetic applications. When each Jewish family was choosing their lamb on the tenth day of Nisan for Passover, God was choosing His Lamb at the triumphant entry of Jesus. On the day and hour that the lamb was being sacrificed at the Temple, Jesus, the Lamb of God, was also being crucified on the cross. This is why the historical observation of the lamb being sacrificed upright on a pole, as Christ was being sacrificed upright on a cross, paints such a meaningful picture.

THE LAMB

Let's take a closer look at the lamb. A number of years ago I heard Jimmy DeYoung, an outstanding news commentator and Bible teacher, teach at a conference. Since it was during the Christmas season, he was teaching about the birth of Jesus in the first chapter of Luke. He read to us Luke 2:8-12: "And in the same region there were some shepherds staying out in the fields, and keeping watch over their flock by night. And an angel of the Lord suddenly stood before them, and the glory of the Lord shone around them; and they were terribly frightened. And the angel said to them, 'Do not be afraid; for behold, I bring you good news of a great joy which shall be for all the people; for today in the city of David there has been born for you a Savior, who is Christ the Lord. And this will be a <u>sign</u> for you: you will find a <u>baby</u> wrapped in <u>cloths,</u> and <u>lying in a manger.</u>'"

He then asked us in the audience a startling question: "Did you ever wonder <u>why this was a sign?</u>" This left us all speechless. I had to admit to myself that I had never even questioned it. Why was it a sign? Dr. DeYoung had us turn to the book of Micah. We were all familiar with Micah 5:2, which prophesied that the Messiah would be born in <u>Bethlehem,</u> but many of us were not familiar with <u>Micah 4:8,</u> which prophesied that He would be <u>announced at the tower of the flock</u> (*Migdal Eder*). Dr. DeYoung, who had lived in Jerusalem for a number of years, told us that Migdal Eder was a two-story tower that had been in the pasture outside Bethlehem. The remains of the place had recently been discovered. He explained that the shepherds in the field had <u>not all been the lowly shepherds</u> which we had always assumed. They were actually <u>priests</u> from the <u>temple</u> who were <u>doing shepherding work</u> to assist in the <u>birthing</u> of the <u>sacrificial lambs</u> so that they would be <u>unblemished</u> for <u>sacrifice</u>. While the shepherds were keeping watch over the flock from the top floor of the tower, the <u>shepherd-priests</u> would bring the <u>pregnant sheep</u> into the bottom floor to <u>take care of the newborn lambs</u>. As soon as the lamb was born, they would <u>wrap the lamb</u> with <u>strips of cloths made from old priestly undergarments.</u> This was <u>done to keep the lamb from getting blemished</u>. They would then <u>place</u> the <u>lamb</u> onto a <u>manger</u> to make sure it would not be trampled. Wow! So when these shepherd-priests went into Bethlehem and saw the baby Jesus wrapped in cloths, lying in a manger, they must have exclaimed, "There is the Lamb of God, prepared for sacrifice, unblemished!" I will presume that his cloths were from the same source as the lambs' cloths. Mary's cousin, Elizabeth, was married to the priest, Zacharias. Elizabeth could have given her the cloths made from the priestly undergarments. What a sign! I was so intrigued by this that I did some further research. These historical observations and parallels were confirmed by many messianic rabbis and the renowned historical writer Alfred Edersheim. I also sought out help from Bob Ibach, an experienced archaeologist, who had done some digs in Israel. He found the written account and pictures of the discovery of "the tower of the flock" (*Migdal Eder*). This whole insight on the account of the announcement of the birth of Jesus was so astounding and exciting.

In my research more and more facts began to unfold. I was talking further with David Schiller, my Jewish teacher and friend, about what I had learned about the shepherds and the lambs. He amazed me with some more historical insights. He explained that each Jewish family would put the family name around the neck of their lamb that they took to the Temple to be sacrificed. They did this to make sure they received their own lamb back for the Passover dinner. I wondered if there was any significance to this piece of trivia. As I was contemplating this, Schiller pointed out to me an interesting object found in most of the paintings of Christ on the cross. There was a small sign at the top of the cross that looked like four letters: "INRI." I discovered that this was an abbreviation of the sign that Pontius Pilot placed on the cross as seen in John 19:19: "And Pilate wrote an inscription also, and put it on the cross. And it was written, 'JESUS THE

NAZARENE, THE KING OF THE JEWS.'" I learned that the letters were the first letters of each of the nouns in the inscription in Latin. I contacted my daughter, Ruth, who was very good with Latin, and asked her to show me the inscription in the Latin Vulgate. That confirmed it: "Iesus Nazarenus Rex Iudaeorum" (INRI).

Then David opened my eyes to an incredible observation. Since the inscription had been in three languages—Latin, Greek, and Hebrew—he translated it for me in the Hebrew language in the English script. I saw before me these words: "Y'Shua HaNatzri V'Melech HaYehudim." I was absolutely stunned when I took the first letters of each of these words. It spelled "YHVH," the name of God! Just like the Jews put their family name on their lamb for sacrifice at the Temple, God put His name on His Lamb for His family, which includes you and me! God gave us so many pictures so we could understand the magnitude of His loving grace!

THE PASSOVER SUPPER

Now we look at the Passover supper. Exodus 12:8 says, "And they shall eat the flesh that same night, roasted with fire, and they shall eat it with unleavened bread and bitter herbs." I learned that the Passover dinners varied slightly from household to household and from different generations, but the main picture and the order of the feast were the same. I consulted the messianic Hagaddah, which gives the order of the Seder and the meaning of each tradition of the feast. There were some aspects of the feast that captured my curiosity. The most interesting was the four different cups of wine and their meaning as a part of the Jewish tradition. The four cups were to remind everyone of the four promises in Exodus 6:6–7: "Say, therefore, to the sons of Israel, 'I am the LORD, and I will bring you out from under the burdens of the Egyptians, and I will deliver you from their bondage. I will also redeem you with an outstretched arm and with great judgments. Then I will take you for My people, and I will be your God; and you shall know that I am the LORD your God, who brought you out from under the burdens of the Egyptians.'"

I discovered that each cup has its own name in order to designate its significance in the remembrance of the respective key phrase in the above promises in Exodus. I also became aware that the names of the cups varied somewhat among different rabbis. I will refer to the names that seem to be most commonly used. The promise that each cup signifies is the most important aspect. The first cup that is taken at the beginning of the observance is often called the "Cup of Blessing or Sanctification." It refers to the phrase, "I will bring you out . . . ." God promises to separate them from Egypt, which also pictures sanctification, being separated from our sin. Just before the meal the second cup is taken, which is called by some the "Cup of Praise," giving praise to God for His promise, "I will deliver you from bondage." After the meal all participants partake of the third cup, which is called "Cup of Redemption." At the Last Supper, Jesus referred to this cup in Matthew 26:28: "For this is My blood of the covenant, which is poured out for many for forgiveness of sins."

This is the cup that we as Christians partake of at communion. We have been partaking of the third cup! The

fourth cup taken at the end of the observance is commonly #4 cup
called the "Cup of the Kingdom." I noticed that Jesus made
a change in the Seder, which He observed as the Last Supper.
He apparently refrained from drinking the fourth cup. We
read in Matthew 26:29, "But I say to you, I will not drink
of this fruit of the vine from now on until that day when I are there ??
drink it new with you in My Father's kingdom." are cups ?!
4

It became obvious that Jesus did not want to drink of
the fourth cup because everything He did was to fulfill
prophecy. Since the kingdom was not to be established yet,
He skipped that cup and sang a hymn and left. I discussed this
in correspondence with Rabbi Michael Short of Phoenix,
Arizona. He confirmed that observation was accurate, but
he said there are two reasons that Jesus did not drink of the
fourth cup. The other reason absolutely astounded me! Rabbi
Short revealed that it had to do with the Jewish wedding
tradition. When a Jewish lad would propose marriage to a
prospective bride, he would offer a cup of wine. If she drank
it, she was accepting the betrothal. He would then inform
her that he was to go to his father's house to prepare a place
for her. When the place or chamber that he spent time
preparing was complete, his father would tell him that it was
time for him to retrieve his bride. The wedding celebration
lasted seven days. After the seven days, the bride and groom
would come out of the chamber to observe a wedding feast
in their honor. The bride and groom would start the feast
by drinking together a cup of wine that was called the "Cup
of Consummation." This cup, according to Rabbi Michael
Short, is the same as the fourth cup of the Seder, "Cup of
the Kingdom!" After the disciples drank of the third cup,
which was also symbolically the "Cup of Betrothal," Jesus
told them that He was going to His Father's house to prepare

21

a place for them. He said, "I go to prepare a place for you. And if I go and prepare a place for you, I will come again, and receive you to Myself; that where I am, there you may be also" (John 14:2–3).

When Christians take the cup in the communion service, we are actually accepting our betrothal to the Lord. In the kingdom, we will drink the "Cup of Consummation" with our Lord at the Marriage Feast of the Lamb. That will be the Kingdom Cup of the Last Supper. In reality, the Last Supper was unfinished. So after a long break, it will resume again with all of us being present in the kingdom to complete it. If Leonardo da Vinci wants to repaint the Last Supper in its completed form, he will have to come up with a mighty big canvas.

Now let us look at the bread that is referred to in the Seder. It is called *matzah*. If you purchase matzah bread at a store, it looks a lot like a large saltine cracker. It actually is bread that has no leaven in it, which gives it the flat, cracker-like appearance. The matzah bread is baked in such a way that it is pierced with tiny holes in rows, giving it a striped appearance, and has brown spots on it like bruises. Since the temple is no longer in existence for sacrificing the lamb, the rabbis ruled that the matzah bread could suffice for the lamb. This fact ties in beautifully with Isaiah 53:5: "But he was *wounded* for our transgressions, he was *bruised* for our iniquities: the chastisement of our peace *was* upon him; and with his *stripes* we are healed" (emphasis mine). The word *wounded* is translated "pierced" in the NASB.

During the Seder, at the head of the table is a pouch called *matzah tosh,* which has three compartments. Each compartment has a piece of matzah in it. The Jews understand that the three compartments refer to Abraham, Isaac, and Jacob. The Christians understand that the compartments refer to the Father, Son, and Holy Spirit. The same picture is accomplished with both understandings. For instance, Abraham was called out of the Chaldees by God, and God the Father, according to Ephesians 1:4–5, called us before the foundation of the world. Likewise, Isaac, on Mount Moriah, pictured substitutionary atonement, the atonement that Jesus provided when He shed His blood for us. Sanctification is illustrated in Jacob's life, as the Holy Spirit provides sanctification in the believer's life. It is a tradition that the matzah in the middle compartment is removed and broken in half. The half piece is called the *afikomen* and is wrapped in a cloth and hidden for later retrieval by the children at the end of the meal. When a child finds the *afikomen*, he is given a gift, usually in the form of money. It reminds me of Ephesians 4:7: "But to each one of us grace was given according to the measure of Christ's gift."

The Greek meaning of *afikomen* is "that which is coming." It can simply refer to dessert, but many take it to mean "he who is coming." According to Jewish tradition, Messiah will come at Passover to bring redemption. This is why a place is left at the table for Elijah, the forerunner of Messiah (Malachi 4:5).

NOTES

NOTES

Chapter 2

THE FEAST OF UNLEAVENED BREAD

The Second of the Spring Feasts

The Feast of Unleavened Bread is an extension of the Passover. "Then on the fifteenth day of the same month there is the Feast of Unleavened Bread to the LORD; for seven days you shall eat unleavened bread" (Leviticus 23:6). Additionally we read in Exodus 12:17–20, "You shall also observe the Feast of Unleavened Bread, for on this very day I brought your hosts out of the land of Egypt; therefore you shall observe this day throughout your generations as a permanent ordinance. In the first month, on the fourteenth day of the month at evening, you shall eat unleavened bread, until the twenty-first day of the month at evening. Seven days there shall be no leaven found in your houses; for whoever eats what is leavened, that person shall be cut off from the congregation of Israel, whether he is an alien or a native of the land. You shall not eat anything leavened; in all your dwellings you shall eat unleavened bread." Starting with Passover and continuing through the next seven days, the Jews are not to eat any leavened bread of any kind. They cannot even have any leavened bread anywhere in their homes or places of business. I have a friend who is a professional photographer. He received a contract to go to Israel to take pictures of various breads at a bakery for an advertisement. We wondered what the bread store would do during the Feast of Unleavened Bread. We had a good chuckle when we found out the answer. The bakery would sell the place to a Gentile for seven days and then buy it back.

BEDIKAT CHAMETZ

There is a curious custom that many Jewish families participate in to prepare for the week of Passover and Feast of Unleavened Bread. It is called *Bedikat Chametz*. This custom is a kind of game to teach the children about how the Lord cleanses us of our sin in our daily walk with Him. The game consists of candles, a wooden spoon, a feather, leavened crumbs of bread, and a furnace of fire. The father of the household gives each child a candle, and they go about their home looking for the leavened crumbs that have been placed in various locations around the house. When the children see a crumb, they call out to their father. He comes and gently brushes the crumb onto the wooden spoon with the feather and carries the crumb to a furnace to be burned. The picture here illustrates that if we walk in the light of God's Word, He shows us our sin. When we call out to our heavenly Father, He gently takes away our sin. The wooden spoon is symbolic of the wooden cross of Christ. This game teaches the children about sanctification. We read in 1 Corinthians 5:7–8: "Clean out the old leaven, that you may be a new lump, just as you are in fact unleavened. For Christ our Passover also has been sacrificed. Let us therefore celebrate the feast, not with old leaven, nor with the leaven of malice and wickedness, but with the unleavened bread of sincerity and truth." The Feast of Unleavened Bread teaches the concept of being in fellowship with the Lord. Believers are to live a sin-free life to maintain fellowship with God. This is done through the continual cleansing by Christ's blood.

Fellowship and Sanctification

In what we call the Upper Room Discourse, Jesus taught Peter the meaning of having continual fellowship with God. We read in John 13:10, "Jesus said to him, 'He who has bathed needs only to wash his feet, but is completely clean; and you are clean, but not all of you.'" The apostle John gives us further explanation of this fellowship that Jesus taught. He says in 1 John 1:7–8, "But if we walk in the light as He Himself is in the light, we have fellowship with one another, and the blood of Jesus His Son cleanses us from all sin. If we say that we have no sin, we are deceiving ourselves, and the truth is not in us." Sin is kept from knocking us out of fellowship with God, since Christ's blood continually cleanses us from all sin. It is the *denial* of the sin that God made us aware, which puts us out of fellowship. If we fall out of fellowship because of denial of convicted sin, and we confess, God restores our fellowship as we see in 1 John 1:9: "If we confess our sins, He is faithful and righteous to forgive us our sins and to cleanse us from all unrighteousness." I consider 1 John 1:7 as maintenance of our fellowship and 1 John 1:9 as restoration of our fellowship.

Speaking of sanctification, the Bible teaches us of four phases of that process. They are preparatory, positional, progressive, and prospective sanctifications. Preparatory sanctification is the process the Holy Spirit uses to bring us to the point of salvation. He worked with us long before we knew Him. 2 Thessalonians 2:13 says, "God has chosen you from the beginning for salvation through sanctification by the Spirit and faith in the truth." Likewise 1 Peter 1:1–2 speaks of those "who are chosen, according to the foreknowledge of God the Father, by the sanctifying work of the Spirit."

Positional sanctification refers to our salvation, the moment we put our faith in Jesus. This is also referred to as justification, when we are declared righteous. 1 Corinthians 1:2 says, "To those who have been sanctified in Christ Jesus, saints by calling." Also we read in Hebrews 10:10, "By His will we have been sanctified through the offering of the body of Jesus Christ once for all."

Progressive sanctification describes the spiritual growth of the believer as he becomes more Christ-like in his walk. This phase is usually what we think of when we refer to sanctification. It is also the phase of sanctification pictured by the Feast of Unleavened Bread. 2 Corinthians 7:1 says,

"Therefore, having these promises, beloved, let us cleanse ourselves from all defilement of flesh and spirit, perfecting holiness in the fear of God." Also 2 Corinthians 3:18 explains, "But we all, with unveiled face beholding as in a mirror the glory of the Lord, are being transformed into the same image from glory to glory, just as from the Lord, the Spirit."

Prospective or ultimate sanctification is what Christians are looking forward to. It is when we receive our new bodies without the sin nature, and truly live without sin. This phase is called glorification. We read about it in Romans 8:29: "For whom He foreknew, He also predestined to become conformed to the image of His Son, that He might be the first-born among many brethren." And in 1 Thessalonians 5:23–24, we read, "Now may the God of peace Himself sanctify you entirely; and may your spirit and soul and body be preserved complete, without blame at the coming of our Lord Jesus Christ. Faithful is He who calls you, and He also will bring it to pass."

I came across the following admonition to Gentile believers at a messianic congregation: "Let your Jewish friends know the matzah of Passover is central to your faith as well, because of the Jewish Messiah, 'the Lamb of God who takes away the sins of the world'" (John 1:29).

TIMING OF CHRIST'S BURIAL

As you can see, there are many pictures about the Messiah in these first two spring feasts. There are many more; we have merely scratched the surface. I believe, though, that the most important parallel of the feasts is the timing of their observance. While Jesus observed the Seder early, His death on the cross occurred at the time the lambs were being sacrificed at the temple. We read in Exodus 12:5–6, "Your lamb shall be an unblemished male a year old; you may take it from the sheep or from the goats. And you shall keep it until the fourteenth day of the same month, then the whole assembly of the congregation of Israel is to kill it at twilight." "Twilight" is also translated in some texts as "between the evenings." This is understood by most Jews as between 3:00 p.m. and 6:00 p.m. Matthew 27:45–50, along with the other gospels, records the death of Jesus on the cross as 3:00 p.m., which parallels in the time the first Passover lambs were being slaughtered. We read in Matthew 27:45–50, "Now from the sixth hour [3:00 p.m.] darkness fell upon all the land until the ninth hour [6:00 p.m.]. And about the ninth hour Jesus cried out with a loud voice, saying, 'ELI, ELI, LAMA SABACHTHANI?' That is, 'MY GOD, MY GOD, WHY HAST THOU FORSAKEN ME?' And some of those who were standing there, when they heard it, began saying, 'This man is calling for Elijah.' And immediately one of them ran, and taking a sponge, he filled it with sour wine, and put it on a reed, and gave Him a drink. But the rest of them said, 'Let us see whether Elijah will come to save Him.' And Jesus cried out again with a loud voice, and yielded up His spirit."

Jesus was buried on the first day of the Feast of Unleavened Bread. Two days before Jesus's crucifixion, He prepared His disciples by saying in Matthew 26:2, "You know that after two days the Passover is coming, and the Son of Man is to be delivered up for crucifixion." We read in John 19:31, "The Jews therefore, because it was the day of preparation, so that the bodies should not remain on the cross on the Sabbath (for that Sabbath was a high day), asked Pilate that their legs might be broken, and that they might be taken away." The "day of preparation" and the "high day," both refer to the Passover. It was a special Sabbath which was also the first day of the Feast of Unleavened Bread. Therefore, this Passover was not referring to a weekly Sabbath. Our sins were paid for on the cross on the fourteenth of Nisan, which was the Passover, and buried with Christ on the fifteenth of Nisan. When things look like they are out of control, we must remember that God is still in control of all things. Paul reiterated this truth when he wrote, in 1 Corinthians 5:7, "For Christ our Passover also has been sacrificed."

NOTES

NOTES

 ————————————————————————

Chapter 3

THE FEAST OF FIRSTFRUITS

The Third of the Spring Feasts

I was astounded that there were so many pictures and parallels in the first two feasts about Jesus Christ and His ministry. I expected that I would find some more surprises with the other two spring feasts: the Feast of Firstfruits and the Feast of Pentecost. I am happy to tell you that I was not at all disappointed. In fact, I was amazed at the information I discovered.

In Leviticus 23:9–11 we read, "Then the Lord spoke to Moses, saying, 'Speak to the sons of Israel, and say to them, "When you enter the land which I am going to give to you and reap its harvest, then you shall bring in the sheaf of the firstfruits of your harvest to the priest. And he shall wave the sheaf before the Lord for you to be accepted; on the day after the Sabbath the priest shall wave it."'" I noticed two things right away. First, the Jews had to be in the Promised Land before they could observe this celebration that we call the Feast of Firstfruits. Second, they obviously could not observe it until the time of the harvest. This led me to study the harvest seasons of Israel. I had no idea that the facts of the harvests would open up a whole new line of discovery. Being a gardener for many years, I am aware of the importance of the stages of the moon in planting and harvesting. I was impressed when I noticed that the planting and harvest cycles of Israel tie in closely with the positions of the moon.

SIGNIFICANCE OF THE MOON TO CROPS

The four stages of the moon are important to raising crops: new moon, second quarter, full moon, and fourth quarter. When I studied forestry in college, I learned that the new moon gravitationally pulls water up through the soil and causes seeds to swell and burst. This makes it the best time to plant grain crops and other plants that are grown for above-ground produce. The increasing moonlight also causes a good balance between the root development and leaf growth. The second quarter produces less gravitational pull, but provides vibrant moonlight. This is very beneficial to leaf growth. On the other hand, after the full moon, the moonlight is waning, but the gravitational pull is strong again. This combination makes it best for planting root crops. The fourth quarter provides less gravitational pull and moonlight. This is more of a resting period, which makes it an opportune time for cultivating and harvesting.

HARVEST PHASE

The harvesting times in Israel occur primarily during the fourth quarter of the moon. Since the feasts of God in Leviticus synchronize with the harvests, they also synchronize with the stages of the moon. The barley harvest is the first major harvest by the Jews. As it has been set up by God, the Feast of Firstfruits is tied to that harvest. For every harvest in Israel there are three phases: firstfruits, general harvest, and gleanings. The phase of firstfruits also has three phases of activity: marking, gathering, and presenting. The marking refers to the activity of identifying the first maturing barley to be bound in a sheaf, usually by a red cord for easy spotting. Then the chosen barley was gathered and bound as a sheaf. The sheaf was brought to the priest to be presented or waved before the Lord at the altar. As we read in Leviticus 23:10–11, "When you enter the land which I am going to give to you and reap its harvest, then you shall bring in the sheaf of the firstfruits of your harvest to the priest. And he shall wave the sheaf before the LORD for you to be accepted; on the day after the Sabbath the priest shall wave it." This process or activity was done on the day after the weekly Sabbath, which fell on the week of the Feast of Unleavened Bread.

In 1 Corinthians 15:20–23, we read about Jesus Christ: "But now Christ has been raised from the dead, the firstfruits of those who are asleep. For since by a man came death, by a man also came the resurrection of the dead. For as in Adam all die, so also in Christ all shall be made alive. But each in his own order: Christ the firstfruits, after that those who are Christ's at His coming." Also James 1:18 says, "In the exercise of His will He brought us forth by the word of truth, so that we might be, as it were, the firstfruits among His creatures." We know that Jesus rose from the dead on the day of the Feast of Firstfruits, because of Luke 24:1–3: "But on the first day of the week, at early dawn, they came to the tomb, bringing the spices which they had prepared. And they found the stone rolled away from the tomb, but when they entered, they did not find the body of the Lord Jesus." We should remember that the Feast of Firstfruits falls on the day after the Sabbath. We are identified with Christ as our firstfruits, because of James 1:18.

THE HARVESTS AND THE RESURRECTIONS

I was astounded to discover that the order of harvests in Israel parallels the order of the resurrections of believers. As we already observed, there is the barley harvest in the early spring. In a process called winnowing, the barley kernels are tossed into the wind to separate the kernels from the chaff. This is done because the head of the barley is very soft and easily crushed. This reminds me of the birth of the church at Pentecost when the Holy Spirit came like a wind and indwelt the believers as reported in Acts 2:1–2. There came a noise like a violent rushing wind that filled the room! In the order of the resurrections, the church is the first to be resurrected, just as the barley is the first to be harvested. It is like the church was winnowed from the world.

In the late spring, the wheat harvest begins. Since the head of the wheat is hard, it must be threshed or crushed to separate the wheat from the chaff. A man who is threshing the wheat stands on a large board, which has bits of glass underneath it, and is pulled by a horse over the wheat to do the crushing. I found it quite telling that the board is called by a Latin word: *tribulum*. Many people, including Jews, will come to Christ in the tribulation, as noted in Revelation 7:9–14. It is interesting that you can also tell the difference between a field of wheat and a field of barley. While the heads of the stock of barley bend down like they are bowing in humility, the heads of the stocks of wheat stay straight up. I am reminded of Deuteronomy 31:27 where Moses said to the children of Israel, "For I know thy rebellion, and *thy stiff neck*: behold, while I am yet alive with you this day, ye have been rebellious against the LORD; and how much more after my death?" The church will be resurrected first (the barley), while those who become believers in the tribulation (the wheat) will be resurrected during the tribulation if they die in that period. In a sense they were harvested under the crushing of the *tribulum*.

At the beginning of the fall season, the fruit harvest is underway. The grapes are picked and then placed in the winepresses. This is parallel to the judgment in Revelation 14:18–20: "'Put in your sharp sickle, and gather the clusters from the vine of the earth, because her grapes are ripe.' And the angel swung his sickle to the earth, and gathered the clusters from the vine of the earth, and threw them into the great wine press of the wrath of God. And the wine press was trodden outside the city, and blood came out from the wine press, up to the horses' bridles, for a distance of two hundred miles." And finally, there is the gleaning. Leviticus

19:9–10 instructs the Jews *not to harvest the corners* of their fields and vineyards in order to leave grain and fruit for the poor. This is similar to Matthew 24:31, when the believers from the four winds of the earth will be gathered at the end of the tribulation to enter the kingdom. Since they did not die, they are *not resurrected*. Instead, they will move into the kingdom to populate it for the next thousand years.

THE PARALLELS WITH CHRIST

Getting back to the events of the Feast of Firstfruits, it is amazing how the Lord fulfilled the particulars of the feast. According to the timing of the selection and gathering of the barley for firstfruits as stated in the Mishna (the collection of oral laws recorded in the Talmud), a parallel with Christ's trial is apparent. About the time Caiaphas, the high priest, was trying Jesus, the servants of the disciples of the Sanhedrin were in the barley field judging the crop to decide which would be harvested for firstfruits. And on the day the Romans were binding up Jesus for crucifixion, the disciples of the Sanhedrin were binding up the barley sheaf for the firstfruits.

We read in John 20:1, "Now on the first day of the week Mary Magdalene came early to the tomb, while it was still dark, and saw the stone already taken away from the tomb." This was the next day after the weekly Sabbath, being the day of the Feast of Firstfruits. John 20:11–12 says, "But Mary was standing outside the tomb weeping; and so, as she wept, she stooped and looked into the tomb; and she beheld two angels in white sitting, one at the head, and one at the feet, where the body of Jesus had been lying." I couldn't help but notice something startling. Can you see it? Do you realize what Mary saw? She was actually seeing a live display of the mercy seat! That is very exciting. "She beheld two angels in white sitting, one at the head, and one at the feet, where the body of Jesus had been lying."

We immediately observe another thing in John 20:17, which had always puzzled me. When Mary recognized the resurrected Lord, He tells her, "Touch me not; for I am not yet ascended to my Father: but go to my brethren, and say to them, I ascend unto my Father, and your Father; and to my God, and your God." I never fully understood why He said that to Mary. Why couldn't she touch Him? I discovered the reason when I read what Flavius Josephus wrote about the barley. He explained that the Jews could not touch the barley before the day of firstfruits. Once the barley sheaf was presented to God by the priest, the barley crop could be harvested for use. Since Jesus was the Firstfruits, He had to go to the Father before anyone could touch Him. We see that after He had been to the Father and back, Thomas could touch Him. As John 20:27 states, "Then He said to Thomas, 'Reach here your finger, and see My hands; and reach here your hand, and put it into My side; and be not unbelieving, but believing.'"

Until they harvested and offered the barley sheaf or *omer* in the temple, the rest of the crops were not deemed kosher (lawfully fit or acceptable). We read a great truth in 1 John 2:2: "And he is the propitiation for our sins: and not for ours only, but also for the sins of the whole world." We are now *kosher*, so to speak, because of what Christ had done on our behalf in fulfilling the Feast of Firstfruits to the very letter! The field of barley became kosher by the firstfruits being presented to God at the temple. The barley in the field did nothing to become kosher. In the same way, we have been made acceptable to God by Jesus, our Firstfruits, when He presented Himself to the Father. As the barley in the field did nothing to become kosher, likewise, we did nothing to become kosher.

We have observed in the events of history, it was by God's design that the activity of marking, gathering, and presenting the barley sheaf of Firstfruits coincided exactly with the death and resurrection of Christ. Why don't the Jews see the parallel? Many may be blinded now, but a day will come when they will see. This was promised in Zechariah 12:10: "And I will pour out on the house of David and on the inhabitants of Jerusalem, the Spirit of grace and of supplication, so that they will look on Me whom they have pierced; and they will mourn for Him, as one mourns for an only son, and they will weep bitterly over Him, like the bitter weeping over a first-born."

NOTES

NOTES

Chapter 4

THE FEAST OF PENTECOST

The Fourth of the Spring Feasts

The parallels and contrasts which are evident in the Feast of Pentecost of the New Testament with the Feast of Weeks of the Old Testament are also startling. The Feast of Weeks in the Old Testament is the same feast the disciples observed in the New Testament, known as the Feast of Pentecost. At the first Feast of Weeks, God provided the law. God had given them freedom from bondage and slavery, so He then gave them the law to guide them in living. As slaves they were told what to do by their masters, but in freedom they needed guidance from their new Master, the Lord God of heaven. It should be noted that God gave them freedom, salvation from slavery, before He gave them the law. Keeping the law was not a condition for receiving their freedom but a response to God's grace of setting them free. At the first Feast of Pentecost in the New Testament, God provided His Holy Spirit for guidance. The Feast of Weeks/Pentecost is celebrating God's provisions for life. It is observed during the time of the wheat harvest, a major provision of the Lord. In Leviticus 23:15–16 God told the Jews, "You shall also count for yourselves from the day after the sabbath, from the day when you brought in the sheaf of the wave offering; there shall be seven complete sabbaths. You shall count fifty days to the day after the seventh sabbath; then you shall present a new grain offering to the Lord."

A new grain offering was to be offered again. But what is different with this offering is spelled out in the very next verse: "You shall bring in from your dwelling places two loaves of bread for a wave offering, made of two-tenths of an ephah; they shall be of a fine flour, baked with leaven as firstfruits to the Lord." Leaven is now introduced to the bread in place of the unleavened bread of the former feasts. But why? Checking with the messianic rabbis, I discovered a logical answer to this question. While the Passover is referring to God and the purging of sin, the Feast of Weeks or Pentecost refers to God's people who receive the law and the Spirit. We still have sin in our lives until we receive our new glorified bodies at the rapture. We read in 1 Corinthians 10:17, "Since there is one bread, we who are many are one body; for we all partake of the one bread." The two loaves mentioned in Leviticus 23:17 picture the Jew and the Gentile, but we are now one body, "one loaf." There is a number of other offerings and sacrifices that are presented at the temple at this time as well, and they are applied to several things from sins to thanksgivings.

COUNTING OF THE OMER

According to Leviticus 23:15–16, the Jews were commanded to start counting fifty days from the day of the Feasts of Firstfruits to the next feast, the Feast of Weeks/ Pentecost. During the forty-nine days of this count, which they call "counting of the omer," the wheat crop is in the ripening process. By the end of the omer count, the crop is ready for harvest, and the firstfruits of the wheat crop can be brought to the temple for Pentecost on the fiftieth day. Shavuot, the Hebrew name for this festival, means "seven weeks." This concludes the festival season, which began at Passover. Just as Firstfruits celebrate the ripening of the barley crop, Shavuot celebrates the ripening of the wheat crop.

THE REMEMBRANCES

The feasts all have a historical significance. Pesach is a remembrance of the slaying of the Passover Lamb. The first day of Unleavened Bread is a remembrance of the exodus from Egypt. Shavuot is a remembrance of the giving of the law at Mount Sinai. The seventh day of Passover, according to tradition, remembers the crossing of the Red Sea. The counting of the omer is regarded as a remembrance of the intervening days between the exodus from Egypt and the revelation at Sinai. Therefore, Shavuot became known as the anniversary of God's appearance at Mount Sinai.

On the first Pentecost (Weeks), signs and wonders accompanied the giving of the Torah at Mount Sinai. Smoke, fire, and clouds were on the mountain. The mountain trembled and the blast of a shofar sounded louder and louder. The voice of God was audibly heard by the entire nation. The midrash, a collection of Jewish oral traditions of the things that happened in history, comments on Exodus 20:18 about flames of fire at Sinai, "On the occasion of the giving of the Torah, the children of Israel not only heard the LORD's voice, but actually saw the sound waves as they emerged from the LORD's mouth. They visualized them as a fiery substance. Each commandment that left the LORD's mouth traveled around the entire camp and then came back to every Jew individually. And all the people witnessed the thunderings. Note that it does not say *the thunder*, but *the thunderings*. Rabbi Johanan said that God's voice, as it was uttered, split up into seventy voices, in seventy languages, so that all the nations should understand."

In this same section of the midrash it says, "God came down from the heavens, and stepped onto the top of Mount Sinai. There was wind, lighting, thunder, fire, smoke; and there was the very loud sound of a ram's horn trumpet blowing. And apparently the entire camp audibly heard the voice of God speaking the Ten Commandments!" It says in Exodus 19:16, "So it came about on the third day, when it was morning, that there were thunder and lightning flashes and a thick cloud upon the mountain and a very loud trumpet sound, so that all the people who were in the camp trembled." The parallels are quite fascinating when we read in Acts 2:2–6, "And suddenly there came from heaven a noise like a violent, rushing wind, and it filled the whole house where they were sitting. And there appeared to them tongues as of fire distributing themselves, and they rested on each one of them. And they were all filled with the Holy Spirit and began to speak with other tongues, as the Spirit was giving them utterance. Now there were Jews living in Jerusalem, devout men, from every nation under heaven. And when this sound occurred, the multitude came together, and were bewildered, because they were each one hearing them speak in his own language."

We can't prove everything that the midrash says happened, but we can assume that all the people who were in the room in Acts 2 were familiar with it. They could immediately make the connection of the events in the Feast of Weeks of the Old Testament with those in the Feast of Pentecost in the New Testament.

FILLING OF THE SPIRIT

The concept of the filling of the Spirit has always drawn different opinions of what it really is. One thing I observed about filling was that in the Greek there are two different words for the process. In Ephesians 5:18 the word of *filling* is *pleroo*, which has the idea of growth to maturity or being molded by the Word of God. If we compare Ephesians 5:18 with Colossians 3:16, which is discussing the same subject, we can see that "be filled with the Spirit" is the same as "Let the word of Christ richly dwell within you." Since this command is in the present tense, this indicates a continual experience or process. Both phrases have the same result. On the other hand, *pimplemi* in Acts 2:4 is in the aorist tense, which indicates a single event or happening. In context, the word implies an empowering for a work of service. The event also describes or alludes in context to the phenomenon of the baptism of the Holy Spirit. Today, since the Spirit indwells us as believers, we can be empowered by the Holy Spirit in our respective ministries. So the Holy Spirit is doing two major things for us: empowering and maturing us. It is also interesting to note that when Paul wrote in 1 Corinthians 6:19, "Do you not know that your body is a temple of the Holy Spirit who is in you," he used the Greek word *naos*, which means "the inner most holy place of the Temple where God dwelt." The other word for temple, *hieron*, means "the entire temple."

FURTHER OBSERVATIONS

I was also intrigued by one important contrast between the Old Testament Feast of Weeks and the New Testament Feast of Pentecost. In Exodus 32:28, we find that three thousand men died that day, but in Acts 2:41 we read that three thousand people were saved. The law brought death, while the Spirit brought life!

It is interesting that the entire Godhead was involved in the fulfilling of the spring feasts. The *Son* honored and fulfilled the Passover by His death. The *Father* honored and fulfilled the firstfruits by raising up Christ from death and the grave. The *Holy Spirit* honored and fulfilled the Weeks by His descent fifty days after the resurrection of Christ. Now we, in response to the fulfilling work of the total Godhead, can truly serve the Lord in all power and truth!

NOTES

NOTES

 ————————————————————————————

Chapter 5

THE FEAST OF TRUMPETS

The First of the Fall Feasts

In studying and researching the historical and spiritual significances of the spring feasts and how Jesus fulfilled them, I was intrigued at how much God had revealed about His plans in these observances. While meditating and sorting out these discoveries, I began to look forward expectantly to what surprising facts lay ahead in studying the fall feasts. Since Jesus fulfilled the spring feasts by the events of His first coming, the parallels and the teachings were obvious once they were noted. I wondered what truths could be gleaned from the fall feasts and how they could be understood, since Jesus has not fulfilled them yet. As I began my study, I was pleased to discover that the fall feasts revealed incredible and exciting facts much like the spring feasts. Just as we have history to look to in the Scriptures for our understanding of the fulfilled feasts, we have prophecy in the Scriptures to draw from to acquire an understanding of the unfulfilled feasts.

Most Christians have probably never studied the Feast of Trumpets, because they may have considered it a Jewish feast with no application to believers today, especially to Gentiles. I have come to the opinion that it is time for Christians to give serious attention to the details of the biblical and traditional aspects of this mysterious feast.

We read in Leviticus 23:24, "Speak to the sons of Israel, saying, 'In the seventh month on the first of the month, you shall have a rest, a reminder by blowing of trumpets, a holy convocation.'" What is the purpose of this blowing of the trumpets, and what is this reminder? Not much was written in the Bible about this observance, so I looked at the Jewish traditions to see if they would shed some light on the subject. Again I was astounded at what was revealed about Christ in those extra-biblical traditions!

To the Jews the most important aspect of this festival is that it is the Jewish New Year. It falls on the first day of Tishri, the seventh month of the Hebrew lunar calendar. It is also very significant in that it is the only feast that falls on the new moon. I will explain that later in this chapter.

On this day, Jewish families enjoy the delicious tradition of eating slices of apples that have been dipped in honey. This is full of meaning to every Jew. They hope the year will be as sweet as the fruit they have eaten. I wondered why apples were chosen as the fruit. I found that the answer is rooted in the Talmud's understanding of Isaac's blessing of Jacob in Genesis 27:27, where Isaac said, "The fragrance of my son is like the fragrance of a field which God has blessed." The Talmud identifies this field as an apple orchard. What a beautiful way to remember the biblical blessing that was bestowed on Jacob and all his descendants!

The Jews also refer to Rosh Hashanah, the Hebrew name for the Feast of Trumpets, by other names which have very interesting meanings. They are Yom Teruah (Day of Awakening Blast or Resurrection); Yom Hadin (Day of Judgment); Yom Zikaron (Day of Remembrance); and Yom Hamelech (Day of Coronation of the King). Interestingly, all the names allude to the coming of the Messiah. The trumpets are to announce His coming! The shofar is the trumpet used for this celebration. The shofar is blown to make an announcement or to proclaim what is coming. The Jews use two types of shofars. A small one is a ram's horn, and a larger Yemenite shofar comes from an African antelope called the kudu. One Sunday morning, I was on my way to church where I was to teach about the Feast of Trumpets. It occurred to me at the time that I should have borrowed a shofar from one of the local synagogues so I could show the people what one looked like. About thirty minutes before I was to speak, I happened to mention to a church member that I wished I had a shofar to show. To my complete surprise she excitedly informed me that she had a Yemenite shofar in the trunk of her car! She had it because she was involved in some fundraising events for Israel, and had placed it in her trunk temporarily. It dawned on me that if God can provide the ram, He can certainly provide the ram's horn!

THE SHOFAR BLASTS

I discovered that there were four types of blasts blown during the festival. They are Tekiah, one long blast of alarm; Shevarim, three medium blasts like wailing; Teruah, nine short blasts like crying; and Tekiah Hagedolah, the longest and loudest blast. Let us take a look at each blast as the rabbis understand them.

First, the Tekiah, a three-second sustained note, is the sound of the king's coronation. Rosh Hashanah is the day of appreciating who God is. The Jews then internalize that understanding so that it becomes a living, practical part of everyday reality. In other words, God is all-powerful. God is the Creator. God is the Sustainer. God is the Supervisor. In short God is King of the universe. Rabbi Tzahi Shapira from San Antonio, Texas, a believer in Jesus, explains, "The word Tekiah really means 'to be stuck' or 'to stop or pause.' Hashem is getting our attention. God is trying to stop us and to focus on him." Hashem (literally, "the name") is the name Jews use for Yahweh, in order to avoid dishonoring His name. Rabbi Shapira referred Psalm 46:10 to me: "Cease striving and know that I am God; I will be exalted among the nations, I will be exalted in the earth."

Second, Shevarim, the three-medium, wailing blasts, is the sobbing cry of a Jewish heart yearning to connect, to grow, to achieve. The Jew cries out to God from the depths of his soul. At this moment, his soul stands before the Almighty without any barriers, and he can truly let go. Rabbi Shapira said that shevarim means "to be broken" and is a sound of repentance in Hebrew. This is a time of asking for forgiveness.

Third, Teruah, nine quick blasts in short succession, resembles an alarm clock, arousing one from a spiritual slumber. The shofar brings clarity, alertness, and focus. The Jews say that on Rosh Hashanah they need to wake up and be honest and objective about their lives: who they are, where they've been, and in which direction they're headed. We must remember that this is the Jewish New Year, so they would obviously want to reassess their lives. Rabbi Shapira says, "Teruah, a series of short, staccato notes extending over a period of about three seconds, is a preparation to receive the king! Stand on guard; the king is about to arrive!"

Fourth, Tekiah Hagedolah, the final blast, a very long sound, is a call to come forth or to arise. It literally means the "Big Tekiah" and is the last trumpet of the service. It is the last call to repentance, before the great Day of the Lord. Rabbi Shapira also comments on this. "Tekiah Hagedolah is the final blast in a set, which lasts ten seconds minimum. This is the Tekiah that announces that the king has arrived (see 1 Thessalonians 4). We remember that Yeshua will arrive with a great Tekiah sound."

In this feast, there are one hundred different trumpet blasts blown with the belief that the gates of heaven are opened for the home taking, which sounds like it is alluding to the rapture. The Tekiah and Tekiah Hagedolah are understood as sounds of triumph and joy, while the Shevarim and Teruah in contrast are sounds of pain, suffering, and repentance. The ceremonial blasts have a sequence that is followed exactly the same every time. It is in this order: *Tekiah, Shevarim-teruah, Tekiah; Tekiah, Shevarim, Tekiah; Tekiah, Teruah,* and then a final blast of *Tekiah Hagedolah* is held as long as possible. This arrangement makes thirty sounds for the series, with Tekiah being one note, Shevarim three, and Teruah nine. This grouping of thirty sounds is repeated twice more, making a total of ninety sounds. At the end of these three repetitions, a single formula of ten blasts closes the service, making a total of one hundred sounds altogether. This is to commemorate the one hundred cries of the mother of Sisera, the Canaanite general who did not make it home after being assassinated by Jael (Judges 5:28). Apparently this is to remind the Jews that no one can escape God's judgment for doing harm to His people.

Marji Hughes, a Jewish believer, made a very interesting application of the shofar. She said, "When the horn is removed from the ram, it is hollowed. The sound can only be produced when it is blown into. In the same way, we are told that Yeshua 'emptied himself' (Philippians 2:6–7). It was the Spirit moving through Yeshua, which enabled Him to produce the pure sound of the Father. We too are called to be shofars, as the Spirit of God moves through us. Unlike Yeshua, who emptied Himself, we are hollow by nature, empty of meaning until filled by the breath of God. By God's Spirit in us we become His voice, sounding forth the call to repentance (Matthew 10:20). 'For it is not you who speak, but it is the Spirit of your Father who speaks in you.'" What a beautiful application that is!

In the celebration of the festival, the people recite Micah 7:18–20. After that, the congregations that are near a body of water will take stones with their sins written on them and cast them into the water. This is to help them internalize what Micah says, "Yes, Thou wilt cast all their sins into the depths of the sea."

THE PROPHETIC IMPLICATIONS

What are the prophetic implications of Rosh Hashanah? One of the names attached to the feast is Yom Zikaron, Day of Remembrance. We read in Malachi 3:16–17, "Then those who feared the Lord spoke to one another, and the Lord gave attention and heard it, and a *book of remembrance* was written before Him for those who fear the Lord and who esteem His name. 'And they will be Mine,' says the Lord of hosts, 'on the day that I prepare *My own possession*, and I will *spare them* as a man spares his own son who serves him.'" This seems to be saying that the Lord was eavesdropping on the believers and heard them honor Him. God then said that He would spare them as they were written in a book of remembrance.

What would He spare them from? The next chapter of Malachi describes the horrible time of judgment that will come on the whole earth, which is referred to in the book of Revelation as the great tribulation. We also read in Daniel 12:1, "Now at that time Michael, the great prince who stands guard over the sons of your people, will arise. And there will be a time of distress such as never occurred since there was a nation until that time; and at that time your people, everyone who is found written in the book, will be rescued." The rescued people are also called "My own possession," which means "peculiar treasure or wealth." This expression is used in several other passages of Scripture. We find it in Exodus

19:5: "Now then, if you will indeed obey My voice and keep My covenant, then you shall be *My own possession* among all the peoples, for all the earth is Mine." In Psalm 135:4 we read, "For the Lord has chosen Jacob for Himself, Israel for *His own possession*." And finally 1 Peter 2:9 says, "But you are a chosen race, a royal priesthood, a holy nation, a people for God's *own possession*." The King James Version translates the description "a people for God's own possession" as "a peculiar people." I had always considered that expression as strange. But I discovered that the English word *peculiar* means "private property" and the root word of *peculiar* is the Latin word *pecus,* which means "cattle." In ancient cultures, one's net worth was described in terms of heads of cattle rather than dollars. That is why in Psalm 50:10 we are told that God owns all the cattle on a thousand hills. His wealth is immeasurable. Likewise, we are very valuable to God, so we are *peculiar to Him*.

THE RAPTURE

I discovered that quite a number of observations indicate that the Feast of Trumpets looks prophetically to the rapture. Zola Levitt was the first one to direct me to them. Since the rapture is referring to the church, many believers discount any association of this feast with the rapture. They understand that the feasts in Leviticus are exclusively for Israel. True, the feasts have been given to the Jews, but God said emphatically that they were *His feasts.* They are about Christ's agenda, not Israel's. We already observed that the spring feasts are referring to all aspects of Christ's first coming: His death, burial, and resurrection. Pentecost is applied to the indwelling of the Holy Spirit, which came after the ascension of Christ and came to the Church. On the other hand, the fall feasts refer to the events surrounding Christ's second coming, which also involves the church.

Several reasons make it apparent that the Feast of Trumpets does apply to the rapture. One interesting point, even though somewhat minor, is that the longest gap between two of the feasts is the gap between Pentecost and Trumpets. I believe that alludes to the lengthy time between Christ's two comings. There were months of silence from God between these two feasts without any new revelations, just like the interval between His two comings. Likewise, since Pentecost starts at varied times each year, the days between Pentecost and the Feast of Trumpets vary each year. But most importantly, as mentioned before, Rosh Hashanah (Feast of Trumpets) is the only feast that starts on the new moon. Why is that important? Because, according to the Talmud, the rabbis watch for the appearance of the new moon, because no one knows the day or hour when it will appear! They observe the feast for two days to make sure that they celebrate the feast on the exact day of the new moon, whichever day it would appear.

Also a parallel or picture in the Jewish wedding custom is noteworthy. After a prospective bride accepts the betrothal, the groom goes to prepare a chamber for his bride at his father's house. After the groom finishes preparing the bridal chamber, he must wait for his father to tell him when he can go take his bride. Of course, only the father knows when the proper time will be. In Mark 13:32 Jesus was quoting the typical response of a groom when asked when the wedding would take place. When His disciples asked when He would return, He answered, "But of that day or hour no one knows, not even the angels in heaven, nor the Son, but the Father alone." He was talking to His disciples as His bride!

Now let's take another look at the two most quoted verses about the rapture. In 1 Thessalonians 4:16–17, we read, "For the Lord Himself will descend from heaven with a shout, with the voice of the archangel, and *with the trumpet of God*; and the dead in Christ shall rise first. Then we who are alive and remain shall be caught up together with them in the clouds to meet the Lord in the air, and thus we shall always be with the Lord." Then 1 Corinthians 15:52 says, "In a moment, in the twinkling of an eye, at *the last trumpet*; for the trumpet will sound, and the dead will be raised imperishable, and we shall be changed." What is the last trumpet to which he is referring? It can't be referring to the seventh trumpet of judgment in the book of Revelation, because that book had not been written yet. And the seventh trumpet in Revelation will be in the tribulation and will introduce the seven bowl judgments. No one asked Paul which trumpet he was referring to. They must have all assumed that he was referring to the "Tekiah Hagedolah," the last of the one hundred trumpet blasts of Rosh Hashanah.

Since the spring feasts were fulfilled by Christ each on the exact day and hour, it would stand to reason that the fall feasts would also be fulfilled the same way. Imminency is still intact as a fundamental concept, since we still do not know the day or hour or even the year of the rapture. But God never does anything at random. We may have misinterpreted Mark 13:32 in thinking that the rapture could happen on any day of the year. The messianic Jews, with whom I have had the pleasure of discussing this concept, have all responded to me with this: "Of course the rapture will happen at Rosh

Hashanah!" Clearly the church age started at the Feast of Pentecost, and apparently it will end at the last trumpet blast of the Feast of Trumpets in the year God the Father has planned. We still do not know which day, hour, or year of the two-day feast that it will occur. All we can do is follow the admonition of our Lord and Savior: "And what I say unto you I say unto all, 'Watch'" (Mark 13:37). We watch by observing the signs of the times.

NOTES

NOTES

Chapter 6

THE DAY OF ATONEMENT

The Second of the Fall Feasts

The Day of Atonement (Yom Kippur) follows closely after Rosh Hashanah. We read in Leviticus 23: 26–28, "And the Lord spoke to Moses, saying, 'On exactly the tenth day of this seventh month is the Day of Atonement; it shall be a holy convocation for you, and you shall humble your souls and present an offering by fire to the Lord. Neither shall you do any work on this same day, for it is a day of atonement, to

make atonement on your behalf before the Lord your God.'"
And Exodus 30:10 says, "And Aaron shall make atonement
on its horns once a year; he shall make atonement on it
with the blood of the sin offering of atonement once a year
throughout your generations. It is most holy to the Lord."
The Jews consider the Day of Atonement the holiest day in
all, for it is on this day that Israel would be forgiven of their
sins or would face judgment. Devout Jews tell me that this
day understandably brings plenty of anxiety into their hearts.
Isn't it wonderful that we believers in our Lord and Savior
Jesus Christ have the peace and assurance that our sins are
forgiven eternally, because of what He has done on the cross!
Yom Kippur literally means "Day of Covering." The word
Kippur also means "ransom." It is to show God's willingness
to cover the sins of the previous year.

Leviticus 16:9 gives further instructions on how the Jews
were to observe the Yom Kippur: "On the tenth day of the
seventh month *you must deny yourselves* and not do any work."
In explaining what must characterize the act of denying
oneself, the rabbis say one must avoid eating and drinking,
bathing or washing, marital relations, putting on perfumes
or lotions, and wearing leather shoes. Now "refraining from
the wearing of leather shoes" threw me. I asked about it and
was informed that wearing leather shoes signified luxury.
They wear comfort socks instead.

According to Leviticus 16:31–33, the high priest was to
put on his linen garments and was to make atonement for the
Most Holy Place, the tent or temple, the altar, himself (high
priest), the priests (Levites), and the people (Israelites)—all
in that order. Leviticus 16:3–4 states, "Aaron shall enter the
holy place with this: with a bull for a sin offering and a ram

for a burnt offering. He shall put on the holy linen tunic, and the linen undergarments shall be next to his body, and he shall be girded with the linen sash, and attired with the linen turban (these are holy garments). Then he shall bathe his body in water and put them on." This is not the colorful robe the high priest usually wore. This observance was to be performed once a year according to Leviticus 16:34: "This is to be a lasting ordinance for you: Atonement is to be made once a year for all the sins of the Israelites." The procedure had four parts as spelled out in Leviticus 16:13–14: take fire from the altar of incense, offer sacrifices and place the blood of these sacrifices in a bowl, sprinkle the blood in the Holy Place and upon the mercy seat of the Ark seven times, and then come out and announce, "It is done." The ingredients of the incense are found in Exodus 30:34: "Then the LORD said to Moses, 'Take for yourself spices, stacte and onycha and galbanum, spices with pure frankincense; there shall be an equal part of each.'"

THE SCAPEGOAT

One of the most important aspects of the observance of the Day of Atonement was the scapegoat. We read in Leviticus 16:7–8, "And he shall take the two goats and present them before the Lord at the doorway of the tent of meeting. And Aaron shall cast lots for the two goats, one lot for the Lord and the other lot for the scapegoat." Then verses 9–10 add, "Then Aaron shall offer the goat on which the lot for the Lord fell, and make it a sin offering. But the goat, on which the lot for the scapegoat fell, shall be presented alive before the Lord, to make atonement upon it, to send it into the wilderness as the scapegoat." Laying both hands on the head of the goat, the high priest then confessed the sins of the people. After that he sent the goat away to the wilderness by an appointed person. This fulfills the requirement explained in Leviticus 16:22: "And the goat shall bear on itself all their iniquities to a solitary land; and he shall release the goat in the wilderness." This also ties into Isaiah 53:6, which says, "All of us like sheep have gone astray, each of us has turned to his own way; but the Lord has caused the iniquity of us all to fall on Him."

The Talmud, Tractate Shabbat Folio 86a, states, "How do we know that a crimson-colored strap is tied to the head of the goat that is sent [to 'Azaz'el]? Because it is said, 'If your sins be as scarlet, they shall be as white as snow (Isaiah 1:18).' By a miracle this crimson-colored strap turned white, thus showing the people that they were forgiven of their sins." It then explains, "Rabbi Ishmael says, 'Now did they not have another sign? There was a crimson thread tied to the door of the sanctuary. When the goat had reached the wilderness, the thread would turn white, as it says, "Though your sins be as scarlet, they shall be white as snow."'"

That is fascinating, but this becomes totally amazing when in another section of the Talmud, Yoma 39b says, "Our Rabbis taught: 'During the last forty years before the destruction of the Temple the lot ['For the Lord'] did not come up in the right hand; nor did the crimson-colored strap become white . . . and the doors of the Hekal would open by themselves.'" After Christ was crucified, the crimson strap on the scapegoat and the crimson thread on the temple door never turned white again. Apparently God was reminding the Jews that Jesus is the true Scapegoat once for all. Jesus fulfilled the promise of both goats. He paid the penalty of our sins and removed our sins as well! Since the lot that was drawn for the goat for sacrifice to the Lord never came up in the right hand, this too was a sign that God did not accept their offering again. Hebrews 9:11–12 says, "But when Christ appeared as a high priest of the good things to come, He entered through the greater and more perfect tabernacle, not made with hands, that is to say, not of this creation; and not through the blood of goats and calves, but through His own blood, He entered the holy place once for all, having obtained eternal redemption."

As already noted above, the Talmud says that the temple doors were found open by themselves each evening. In his writings, *The Wars of the Jews,* Josephus said, "At the same festival (Passover) . . . the Eastern gate of the inner court of the Temple, which was of brass, and vastly heavy, and had been with difficulty shut by twenty men, and rested upon a base armored with iron, and had bolts fastened very deep into the firm floor, which was there made of one entire stone, was seen to be opened of its own accord, about the sixth hour of the night." This is similar to the tearing of the veil, which is a sign that there is now total access to God because of the redemptive work of Christ.

THE OBSERVANCES OF YOM KIPPUR

According to Jewish tradition, the observance of Yom Kippur today consists of five services. They are (1) Kol Nidre (the evening service): confessional chant; (2) Shacharit (the early morning service): reading of Leviticus 16 in the temple; (3) Musaf (the second service): reading of the Day of Atonement; (4) Mincha (the afternoon service): reading of Jonah; (5) Ne'ila (the final service): closing or locking the books. I find it interesting that the book of Jonah is read, because Christ said that Jonah was a sign. We read in Luke 11:29–30, "And as the crowds were increasing, He began to say, 'This generation is a wicked generation; it seeks for a sign, and yet no sign shall be given to it but the sign of Jonah. For just as Jonah became a sign to the Ninevites, so shall the Son of Man be to this generation.'"

Another tradition that was started because the temple sacrifices were discontinued was the Kapparot. In this ceremony, a devout Jewish man takes a white rooster, holds it by the right hand, and swings it over his head three times while reciting this prayer: "This fowl shall be in my stead, shall be my atonement; it shall go to death, so that I can attain a good life and peace." This is so sad that their hearts yearn for forgiveness, and yet many Jews have not yet found it in Jesus.

THE PROPHETIC IMPLICATIONS

The heavenly events during the tribulation as described in the book of Revelation gives the impression that Christ is acting out Yom Kippur. The first parallel to note is the period of silence. According to tradition, the high priest was in the Most Holy Place for about half an hour during the sacrifices of Yom Kippur. All the other priests in the temple were waiting in silence for the outcome of the finished sacrifice and the atonement. A parallel in prophecy is seen in Revelation 8:1, which says, "And when He broke the seventh seal, there was silence in heaven for about half an hour." Jesus as our high priest was apparently fulfilling the activities of Yom Kippur at the heavenly temple. We clearly see that from the next two verses, which say, "And another angel came and stood at the altar, holding a golden censer; and much incense was given to him, that he might add it to the prayers of all the saints upon the golden altar which was before the throne. And the smoke of the incense, with the prayers of the saints, went up before God out of the angel's hand. And the angel took the censer; and he filled it with the fire of the altar and threw it to the earth; and there followed peals of thunder and sounds and flashes of lightning and an earthquake." The parallel obviously is the incense at the altar of God. Finally, we see a clear parallel of completion when we read Revelation 16:17: "And the seventh angel poured out his bowl upon the air; and a loud voice came out of the temple from the throne, saying, 'It is done.'" As I mentioned before, after all the sacrifices have been completed on the altar of the Most Holy Place, the high priest would come out and declare, "It is done."

The correlation between the first two fall feasts, Rosh Hashanah and Yom Kippur is startling. The days between Rosh Hashanah and Yom Kippur are called "the Days of Awe." To the Jewish mind, these days are the last chance to find forgiveness from God. After two days of Rosh Hashanah, the high priest (along with the other priests) goes into hiding for seven days to avoid defilement. The next day after the completion of the seven days is the judgment of the Day of Atonement. This paints a great picture of the future when we, as believers as a kingdom of priests, will be in heaven with our High Priest, Jesus Christ, for seven years.

Also another picture is seen in the custom of the Jewish wedding. When the groom brings his bride to the bridal chamber, which he prepared for her in his father's house, they celebrate their union for seven days before the wedding feast. We, as His bride, will be with Christ, our bridegroom, for seven years at the place He has prepared for us at His Father's house. After those seven years, we will return with our Lord as He administers judgment on the earth and salvation to believing Israel, thereby fulfilling Yom Kippur! "And I saw heaven opened; and behold, a white horse, and He who sat upon it is called Faithful and True; and in righteousness He judges and wages war. And His eyes are a flame of fire, and upon His head are many diadems; and He has a name written upon Him which no one knows except Himself. And He is clothed with a robe dipped in blood; and His name is called The Word of God. And the armies which are in heaven, clothed in fine linen, white and clean, were following Him on white horses" (Revelation 19:11–14).

The judgment and salvation which Jesus brings to earth in fulfillment of Yom Kippur are explained in the next two verses: "And from His mouth comes a sharp sword, so that with it He may smite the nations; and He will rule them with a rod of iron; and He treads the wine press of the fierce wrath of God, the Almighty. And on His robe and on His thigh He has a name written, 'KING OF KINGS, AND LORD OF LORDS.'" Also Zechariah 12:10 reads, "And I will pour out on the house of David and on the inhabitants of Jerusalem, the Spirit of grace and of supplication, so that they will look on Me whom they have pierced; and they will mourn for Him, as one mourns for an only son, and they will weep bitterly over Him, like the bitter weeping over a first-born." Their eyes will be open to the truth about Jesus, when He returns!

I came across this heartbreaking quote from Rabbi Yochanan Ben-Zakkai of the Yavneh Council. The Yavneh Council was the council of rabbis that determined the procedures to be followed after the temple was destroyed so traditions would still be intact for future generations. He said in the Talmud in *B'rakhot 28b*, "Now I am being led before the Supreme King of Kings, the Holy One, blessed be He, who lives and endures for ever and ever. If He is angry with me, He is angry forever. If He puts me to death, He puts me to death forever. I cannot persuade Him with words or bribe Him with money. Moreover, there are two ways ahead of me: one leads to paradise and the other to hell, and I do not know which one will take me. How can I do anything but weep?"

How incredibly heart-wrenching that is! This must be the inner cry of every devout Jew, who has not found forgiveness and peace in Jesus.

NOTES

NOTES

Chapter 7

THE FEAST OF TABERNACLES

The Third of the Fall Feasts

THE THIRD OF THE FALL FEASTS

The Feast of Tabernacles, the last of the fall feasts, is just as amazing as the others. Since I was so overwhelmed at how much information God placed in the traditions of the Rosh Hashanah and Yom Kippur, I should not have been surprised that this feast is likewise immensely full of insights about God's plans. But I must confess that I was just as overcome by my amazement at the magnitude of what God revealed in this fascinating festival because like the other feasts, this one too has prophetic implications as well as historical and spiritual significance. The Hebrew word for the feast is *sukkot,* which means "booths."

We are first introduced to the Feast of Tabernacles or Booths in Leviticus 23:33–36, which says, "Again the Lord spoke to Moses, saying, 'Speak to the sons of Israel, saying, "On the fifteenth of this seventh month is the Feast of Booths for seven days to the Lord. On the first day is a holy convocation; you shall do no laborious work of any kind. For seven days you shall present an offering by fire to the Lord."'" This seventh feast, Sukkot, given to Israel is observed from the fifteenth to the twenty-second of Tishri. During this time, many Jewish families construct a *sukkah,* a hastily built hut in which meals are eaten throughout the festival. The sukkah was used to help the people remember the huts Israel lived in during their forty years in the wilderness after their exodus from Egypt. In time they developed a custom of decorating the huts or booths with hanging fruits and other ornaments. It is interesting that America apparently celebrated Sukkot in its early history. In 1621 when the pilgrims gathered to give thanks to the Lord for their first fall harvest, it is understood that they actually celebrated Sukkot, or used it as a model for the celebration of thanks to the Lord for the harvest. This eventually became the holiday of Thanksgiving in 1863.

For forty days from the first of Elul to the tenth of Tishri of the Hebrew calendar, Moses stayed on Mount Sinai a second time. After this period called *Teshuvah* ("repentance"), Moses descended the mountain and gave instructions regarding the building of *God's* Sukkah (the tabernacle). The people then gathered the materials for its construction from Yom Kippur to Sukkot. Interestingly the Jews in our times also start preparing for Sukkot right after they finish observing Yom Kippur.

THE CONCEPT OF JOY

In contrast to Yom Kippur, the Feast of Tabernacles is a season of great joy. In fact, *joy* is a predominant feature of the feast. The people were to be joyful for all that God had provided for them from the harvests of grain and fruit. The Passover, Pentecost, and Tabernacles are often referred to as the pilgrim feasts, because all the males each year were to appear before the Lord in the place where God chose, according to Deuteronomy 16:16–17. At the Passover, though, "joy" is not mentioned. And *joy* occurs only once in the instructions on the Feast of Pentecost. But when we come to Sukkot, *joy* is mentioned twice. In Deuteronomy 16:13–15 we read, "You shall celebrate the Feast of Booths seven days after you have gathered in from your threshing floor and your wine vat; and you shall rejoice in your feast . . . because the Lord your God will bless you in all your produce and in all the work of your hands, so that you shall be altogether joyful." This all makes sense when we look at these three feasts from the agricultural perspective. Passover is the planting season, Pentecost is the wheat harvest-time, and the Feast of Tabernacles is the fruit harvest-time. When all the harvest seasons were complete, there was much rejoicing, and the feast was also called the Feast of Ingathering. When we look at the Feast of Tabernacles, from the spiritual perspective, we can see that it has three purposes for the people. First, it brought joy that their sins were forgiven (during Yom Kippur). Second, it reminded them of God's provision and presence during the Exodus. Third, it reminded them that God was still present and provided for all their needs.

THE TRADITIONS OF THE BUILDING OF THE SUKKAH

God gave the Jews three key instructions for celebrating Sukkot. We find the first instruction in Leviticus 23:40: "Now on the first day you shall take for yourselves the fruit of beautiful trees, palm branches and boughs of leafy trees and willows of the brook; and you shall rejoice before the Lord your God for seven days." They are to gather the "four species." We see the second instruction in Leviticus 23:42: "You shall live in booths for seven days; all the native-born in Israel shall live in booths." They were to live in a hut or *sukkah*. The third instruction is found in Deuteronomy 16:13–14: "You shall celebrate the Feast of Booths seven days after you have gathered in from your threshing floor and your wine vat; and you shall rejoice in your feast, you and your son and your daughter and your male and female servants and the Levite and the stranger and the orphan and the widow who are in your towns." They were to rejoice before the Lord.

The rabbis have added some more instructions for the construction of the sukkah. I have found eight instructions described by John Parsons, a teacher and author on Jewish topics:

1. Choose a site with nothing hanging above it.

2. The floor must be large enough to sit at a table.

3. The walls can be of any material so long as it can withstand normal wind.

4. The roof must be of material that grows from the ground.

5. The roof must give shade in day and allow the viewing of stars at night.

6. It can be decorated with hanging fruits, flowers, popcorn wreaths, ornaments, etc. from the ceiling.

7. Posters of Jewish themes can be taped to the walls.

8. Christmas tree lights hung outside are acceptable.

The Ceremony of the Festival

When Jews today celebrate the Feast of Tabernacles, they recite a blessing on the first night, and then they light two candles. The blessing is this: "Sanctify us, Lord our God, King of the universe, who blessed the holiday of light to kindle and command us with His mitzvoth. Blessed are You, Lord our God, King of the universe, for keeping us alive, taking care of us, and bringing us to this time."

According to the *Encyclopedia Britannica,* a *mitzvoth* is "any commandment, ordinance, law, or statute contained in the

Torah (first five books of the Bible) and, for that reason, to be observed by all practicing Jews." Before the meal Kiddush (sanctification) is recited, and then blessing over the sukkah is said again: "Sanctify us, Lord our God, King of the universe, who blessed us to dwell in the sukkah, and commanded us with His mitzvoth." Traditionally the meal includes stuffed cabbage dishes and fruit or fresh vegetable turnovers. The host of the celebration invites imaginary guests to the meal. Abraham is invited to attend the first night, and then Isaac, Jacob, Joseph, Moses, Aaron, and King David are invited the following nights. Another aspect of the observance is the waving of what is called a *lulav*. This is a bouquet that is made from palm, myrtle, and willow branches and bound together so it can be waved in praise of the Lord. The instructions are to first bind the branches together—two willows on the left, one palm branch in the center, and three myrtles on the right. Next, the bundle is to be held in the right hand. They are also to hold an *etrog*, a lemon-like citrus fruit (pointing downward) in the left hand and to lift them together while reciting the blessing, "Blessed are You, Lord our God, King of the universe, for keeping us alive, taking care of us, and bringing us to this time." While they recite the blessing, they are then to turn the etrog right side up, and, with both hands side by side, shake the lulav three times in each direction: front, right, back, left, up, and down. These six directions indicate the all-encompassing presence of God.

The etrog, branches of palm trees, myrtle, and willows of the brook are considered the four organic products God instructed them to use in Leviticus 23:40. I asked several sources what might be the reasons for their using these four things. The most feasible reasons I found were as follows: the palm branches reminded them of the valleys and plains;

the boughs of trees reminded them of the bushes on the mountain heights; the willows reminded them of the brooks; and the etrog reminded them of the fruits of the land God gave them. The lulav is also shaken during the reading of the praise psalms in the morning service. A hymn that asks to "save us" is also sung. When the weekly Sabbath arrives, Ecclesiastes is read. Possibly this was to remind them that life makes sense only when one trusts the Lord. Psalm 118:15 may refer to this festival when it says, "The sound of joyful shouting and salvation is in the tents of the righteous."

Ceremonies of the Temple

When the temple was still present in Jerusalem, the ceremonies that were a part of the Feast of Tabernacles were quite elaborate, according to historians such as Alfred Edersheim. The ceremonies involved water and light, which symbolized various aspects of the presence of God.

Water-Pouring Ceremony

At the temple the high priest would draw water from the Pool of Siloam in a golden pitcher. He would then bring it through the water gate and pour it in a silver basin at the altar. The people would wave their *lulavot* (plural for *lulav*) and sing, "Save now, I pray, O LORD; O LORD, I pray, send now prosperity." During this water ceremony, the high priest would recite Isaiah 12:1–3: "And in that day you shall say, 'O LORD, I will praise you: though you were angry with me, your anger is turned away, and you have comforted me. Behold, God is my salvation; I will trust, and not be afraid: for the LORD is my strength and my song; he also is become my salvation.'" The golden pitcher has been symbolic of the glory of God, while silver has been figurative of purity and righteousness, which can come only from God's salvation and refining of His people. Water in this context is figurative of the outpouring of the Holy Spirit. Isaiah 12:3 says, "Therefore with joy shall you draw water out of the wells of salvation." Interestingly the word translated as "salvation" here is the word *yeshua*. Ezekiel 36:25 makes a clear promise about salvation, using water figuratively: "I will sprinkle clean water on you, and you will be clean."

The rabbis taught that this water-drawing ceremony was more than simply a request for winter rains. It was to illustrate the days of messianic redemption when the waters of the Holy Spirit will be poured out on all Israel (Sukkoth 55). In John 7:37–38, we read about how Jesus responded to the feast in His ministry: "Now on the last day, the great day of the feast, Jesus stood and cried out, saying, 'If any man is thirsty, let him come to Me and drink. He who believes in Me, as the Scripture said, "From his innermost being shall flow rivers of living waters."'"

In the next verse, John explains what Jesus was referring to: "But this He spoke of the Spirit, whom those who believed in Him were to receive; for the Spirit was not yet given, because Jesus was not yet glorified." The Holy Spirit allows us to experience Immanuel, "God with us." But many of the people did not appreciate the words Jesus spoke. The leaders were quite upset when the temple guards refused their order to arrest Jesus. When one of their own, Nicodemus, spoke in Jesus's defense, they responded by saying, "A prophet does not come out of Galilee" (John 7:52). They conveniently ignored Isaiah 9:1–2, which says, "He shall make it glorious, by the way of the sea, on the other side of Jordan, *Galilee* of the Gentiles. The people who walk in darkness will see a great light; those who live in a dark land, the light will shine on them."

THE LIGHT SHOW

After the water ceremony, during the evening, four seventy-five foot tall menorahs were lit up. The priests would put on a light show all night with torch dances, while the Levites sang and played music. The Talmud quotes a rabbi who referred to the light show by saying, "He who has not seen the rejoicing at the show has never seen rejoicing in his life" (Sukkah 5:1). And that brings us to the second Sukkot symbol—light—that Jesus used to point to Himself as the fulfillment of Scripture. God had promised in Isaiah 9:1–2 that a great light would shine out of Galilee. In John 8:12, Jesus said, "I am the light of the world; he who follows Me shall not walk in the darkness, but shall have the light of life."

In John 7:1–9, we read that Jesus' brothers wanted Him to go up to Judea with them to celebrate the Feast of Tabernacles. Jesus responded, "My time is not yet at hand, but your time is always opportune. The world cannot hate you; but it hates Me because I testify of it, that its deeds are evil. Go up to the feast yourselves; I do not go up to this feast because My time has not yet fully come." As discussed in an earlier chapter, Jesus would not do anything openly in relationship to the feasts unless He was fulfilling something. I will make some observations concerning the prophetic implications of

Sukkot. But first I want to make some comments about Jesus' birth in relation to this feast.

JESUS' BIRTH AND SUKKOT

Strong evidence seems to suggest that Jesus was actually born during the Feast of Tabernacles. First, at the time of His birth, lambs and shepherds were in the field. That would not have been the case if the season was during the winter months. Second, three of the festivals, as noted earlier, were called "pilgrimage" festivals. The reason there was no room at the inn for Joseph and Mary was that everyone was heading to Jerusalem apparently to celebrate one of those feasts. This may be why the Romans took advantage of the time to take a census. All accommodations in Bethlehem, a few miles away, also would have been booked up with travelers. Third, John the Baptist was conceived right after his father Zacharias, who was a priest, was serving in the temple. We know when Zacharias was serving in the temple because we know what priestly order he served in, which was Abiyah. 1 Chronicles 24:10, as well as the Talmud, tells us when each of the twenty-four orders of priests would serve in the temple, and for how long. Each order of priests served for one week and during the weeks of the pilgrimage feasts. Each one of the twenty-four orders of priests would begin and end its service in the Temple on the Sabbath (2 Chronicles 23:8, 1 Chronicles 9:25). Starting with the month of Nisan (first month of the Hebrew calendar), we can figure that Zacharias was serving the tenth week of the year, because he had the eighth cycle of temple service as well as the Feast of Unleavened Bread and the Feast of Pentecost. That would mean that John the Baptist probably was conceived about the third week of Sivan when Zacharias returned home.

Luke 1 states that Jesus was conceived by the Holy Spirit six months after Elizabeth became pregnant. Thus Jesus would have been born six months after John. Assuming the usual forty-week term of pregnancy, John, whom Jesus referred to as "The Elijah who was to come before the Messiah," would have been born during Passover. Counting the weeks from the latter part of Sivan, we arrive at the middle of Nisan, the time of the Passover. The Jews believed that Elijah would come on the Passover. This is why they have a place and a cup for Elijah at the Seder dinner. We read about Jesus' teaching about John the Baptist in Matthew 17:10–13: "And His disciples asked Him, saying, 'Why then do the scribes say that Elijah must come first?' And He answered and said, 'Elijah is coming and will restore all things; but I say to you, that Elijah already came, and they did not recognize him, but did to him whatever they wished. So also the Son of Man is going to suffer at their hands.' Then the disciples understood that He had spoken to them about John the Baptist." Now if we count six months from John's birth, we come to the middle of Tishri, the Feast of Tabernacles! Also of interest is the possibility that Jesus may have been conceived on Hanukkah, the festival of lights, by counting back forty weeks from the Feast of Tabernacles. Being conceived on the "festival of lights" and born on the "show of lights," the Feast of Tabernacles, it is quite appropriate for Him to say, "I am the light of the world. Whoever follows Me will never walk in darkness, but will have the light of life" (John 8:12).

THE PROPHETICAL IMPLICATIONS OF SUKKOT

In Jeremiah 23:7–8, the Lord promised, "'Therefore behold, the days are coming,' declares the Lord, 'when they will no longer say, "As the Lord lives, who brought up the sons of Israel from the land of Egypt," but, "As the Lord lives, who brought up and led back the descendants of the household of Israel from the north land and from all the countries where I had driven them." Then they will live on their own soil.'" Ezekiel shed more light when he prophesied in Ezekiel 37:26–28, "And I will make a covenant of peace with them; it will be an everlasting covenant with them. And I will place them and multiply them, and will set My sanctuary in their midst forever. My dwelling place also will be with them; and I will be their God, and they will be My people. And the nations will know that I am the Lord who sanctifies Israel, when My sanctuary is in their midst forever."

The Lord will dwell with His people forever! He will "tabernacle" with us! We will observe the Feast of Tabernacles every year in the kingdom to celebrate this fact. The prophet Zechariah prophesied by saying, "Then it will come about that any who are left of all the nations that went against Jerusalem will go up from year to year to worship the King, the Lord of hosts, and to celebrate the Feast of Booths. And it will be that whichever of the families of the earth does not go up to Jerusalem to worship the king, the Lord of hosts, there will be no rain on them" (Zechariah 14:16–17). While noting that the Feast of Tabernacles looks to the millennial kingdom, I wondered why the feast was five days after Yom Kippur. Was there any significance to the five days? I was reminded that the number five in Biblical numerology stands for *grace*. It is definitely God's grace when He comes to set up His kingdom on earth to live and reign with us!

NUMEROLOGY

Shemini Atzeret (Eighth Day)

Of interest is the fact that eight days are in this seven-day feast! At the end of the Feast of Tabernacles, the Jews were instructed in Numbers 29:35: "On the eighth day you shall have a solemn assembly; you shall do no laborious work." The Babylonian Talmud explains in Sukkah 55b that during the festival of Sukkoth seventy bulls were sacrificed for the seventy nations at the time of the temple, but on the eighth day, Shemini Atzeret, only one bull was sacrificed for Israel alone. Atzeret comes from the Hebrew root, *atzar*, meaning "to hold back or stop." On the eighth day, the Jews would stop and pray for rain for the future harvests, but it also was a more intimate time with the Lord. The number eight has often carried the symbolic meaning of "new beginning." Since the Feast of Tabernacles celebrates the millennial reign of the Lord, the eighth day, being a convocation of its own, looks toward fellowship with God for eternity and a new beginning. Revelation 21:1–2 says, "And I saw a new heaven and a new earth; for the first heaven and the first earth passed away, and there is no longer any sea. And I saw the holy city, new Jerusalem, coming down out of heaven from God, made ready as a bride adorned for her husband." And the following verse continues: "And I heard a loud voice from the throne, saying, 'Behold, the tabernacle of God is among men, and He shall dwell among them, and they shall be His people, and God Himself shall be among them.'"

CONCLUSION

We can see now that God was very careful to inform us of His plans for Christ's intervention in the life of mankind. Because of our ability to see what happened in recorded history about Christ's first coming, we can marvel at how explicitly He fulfilled the pictures displayed in the spring feasts from Passover to Pentecost. Because of the prophecies that God so graciously gave us in the Scriptures, we can also understand how explicitly He plans to fulfill the pictures displayed about His second coming in the fall feasts from the Feast of Trumpets to the Feast of Tabernacles. God's pictures, parallels, and cycles are so impressive that it would seem that anyone who observed them would come to faith in Jesus Christ as his Savior and Messiah. Since many do not respond that way, this shows that the ministry of the Holy Spirit is necessary to bring a person to put his trust in Jesus.

X THE PICTURES FROM THE HARVESTS

In review, it is very interesting that God apparently patterned the order of resurrections after the patterns of the harvests. The rapture of the church can be illustrated by the barley harvest because of the winnowing by the wind, the softness of the shell, and its being in the first harvest season. Those believers who come out of the tribulation are illustrated by the wheat harvest because of the stiff upright neck and the crushing by the tribulum. The resurrection to judgment at the end of the tribulation is illustrated by the fruit harvest and the winepress. And the ushering of the surviving believers out of the tribulation is illustrated by the gleanings because they are not harvested or resurrected but they live on in the millennium in their nonresurrected bodies.

X CHRIST'S FULFILLMENT OF THE FEASTS

As for the spring feasts, Christ has fulfilled each one on the very day of the feasts, as I previously noted. Christ honored and fulfilled the Passover by His death. He honored and fulfilled the Feast of Unleavened Bread by His burial. God the Father honored and fulfilled the Feast of Firstfruits by raising Christ from death and the grave. The Holy Spirit honored and fulfilled the Feasts of Weeks (Pentecost) by His descent fifty days after the resurrection of Christ.

As for the fall feasts, Christ will honor and fulfill the Feast of Trumpets by taking His bride to the Father's house. Christ will honor and fulfill the Day of Atonement by His second advent. He will honor and fulfill the Feast of Tabernacles by

His setting up of the kingdom on earth and dwelling with us. Christ may well fulfill the fall feasts on the exact days of each of the feasts, just as He did on the spring feasts.

OUR RESPONSE

Time is short, and the time of the fulfillment of the fall feasts by Christ's second coming is close upon us. In light of these teachings from the Scriptures, what should be our response? The apostle Peter answered this question eloquently under God's inspiration in 2 Peter 3:14–18: "Therefore, beloved, since you look for these things, *be diligent* to be found by Him in peace, spotless and blameless, and *regard the patience* of our Lord to be salvation; just as also our beloved brother Paul, according to the wisdom given him, wrote to you, as also in all his letters, speaking in them of these things, in which are some things hard to understand, which the untaught and unstable distort, as they do also the rest of the Scriptures, to their own destruction. You therefore, beloved, knowing this beforehand, *be on your guard* lest, being carried away by the error of unprincipled men, you fall from your own steadfastness, but *grow in the grace and knowledge* of our Lord and Savior Jesus Christ. To Him be the glory, both now and to the day of eternity. Amen."

The main thing to remember as we see God's program unfolding for us in His intervention in the history of mankind is these loving words Christ spoke in John 15:15: "No longer do I call you slaves, for the slave does not know what his master is doing; but I have called you friends, for all things that I have heard from My Father I have made known to you."

ABOUT THE AUTHOR

Michael Norten received a ThM from Dallas Theological Seminary in 1974. He has served on the staff of Campus Crusade for Christ, and has served as a Bible instructor, representing several similar-type ministries for over forty years. He was an associate pastor of Lewisville Bible Church in Lewisville, Texas, and served as interim pastor and pulpit supply for a number of churches in North Texas. He has been an independent representative and regional vice president of a financial services company for thirty years.

He resides in Dallas, Texas, with his wife Ann.

CPSIA information can be obtained at www.ICGtesting.com
Printed in the USA
LVOW071025280213

322077LV00004B/33/P

9 781449 734107